"The Lord is my shepherd; I shall not want.
He makes me lie down in green pastures.
He leads me beside still waters.
He restores my soul.
He leads me in paths of righteousness for his name's sake.
Even though I walk through the valley of the shadow of death,
I will fear no evil, for you are with me;
your rod and your staff, they comfort me."

–Psalm 23:1–4, a psalm written by David

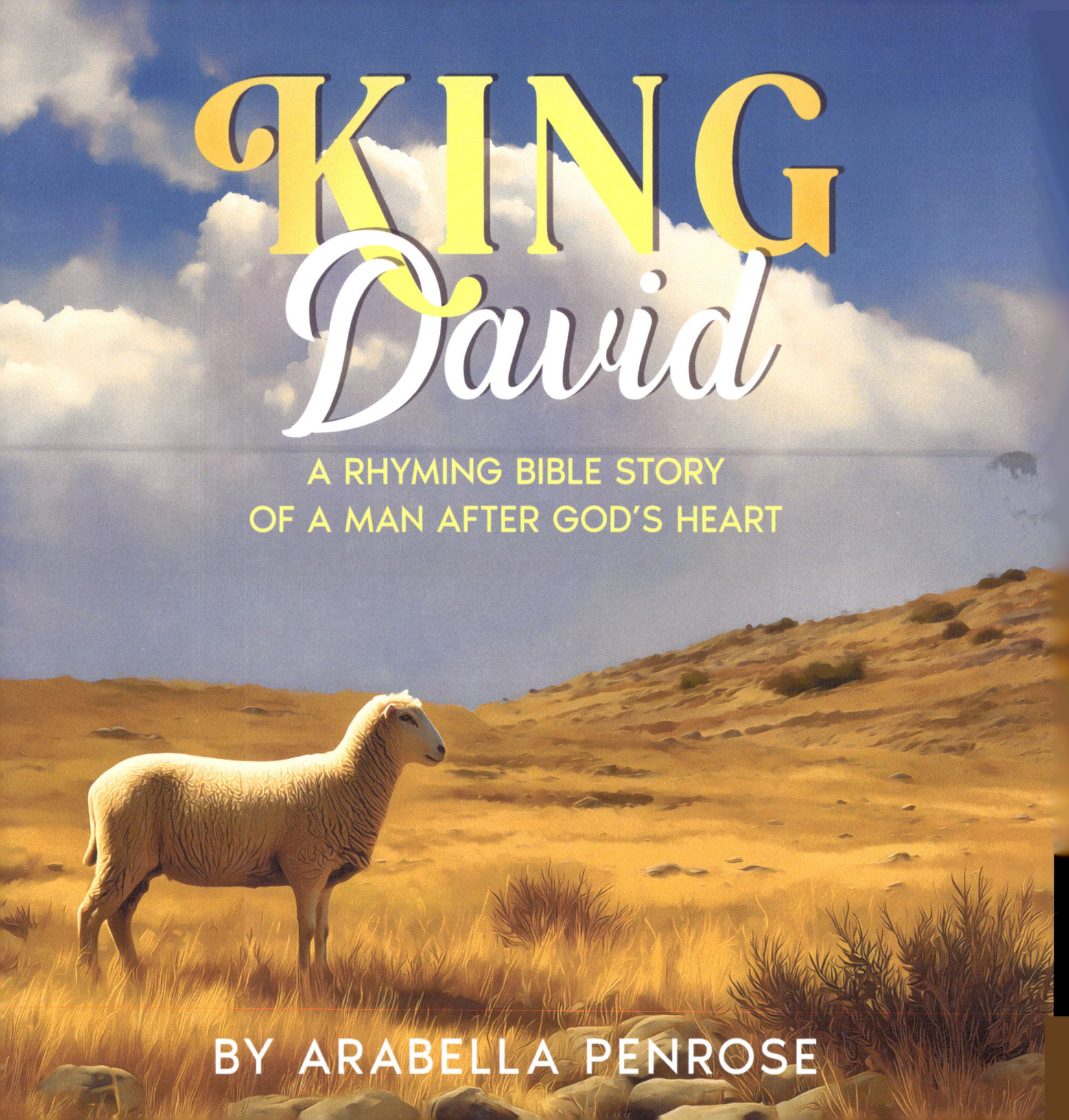

THIS BOOK IS

Presented

TO: _____

BY: _____

ON: _____

Copyright © 2025 Arabella Penrose

Arabella Penrose: Author, Art Director, Book Design
Frank S. Scavo: Poet, Story Editor, Collaborator
Tom B. Free: Artwork Editor

All rights reserved. No part of this publication may be reproduced, distributed, or transmitted in any form or by any means, or stored in any database or retrieval system, without prior written permission of the copyright holder.

All inquiries should be directed to:
www.arabellapenrose.com

ISBN-13: 978-1-962924-11-5 - Paperback
ISBN-13: 978-1-962924-12-2 - Hardcover

Scripture quotations are from The ESV® Bible (The Holy Bible, English Standard Version®), © 2001 by Crossway, a publishing ministry of Good News Publishers. Used by permission. All rights reserved.

For every child with a heart like David's—
May you worship with joy, seek God with faith,
and stay close to Him all your days.

And always remember: Though people
look at the outward appearance,
God sees your heart.

In Bethlehem, so long ago,
Lived David peacefully;
His father Jesse's youngest son,
Belov'd of God was he.

And ev'ry day he'd leave at dawn,
His father's sheep to tend.
At night he'd play upon his harp
And sing to God, his friend.

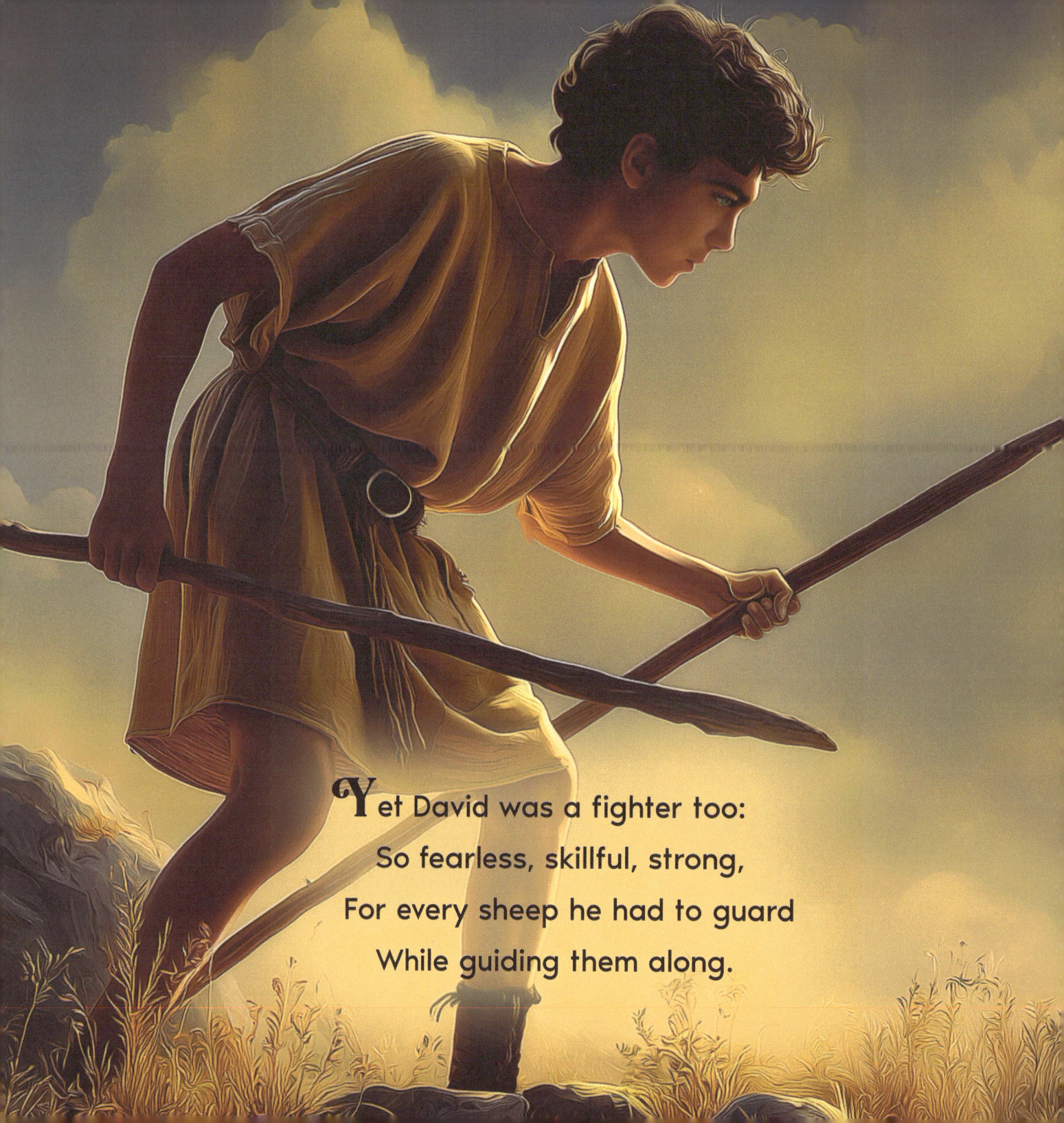

Yet David was a fighter too:
So fearless, skillful, strong,
For every sheep he had to guard
While guiding them along.

Whenever one be taken by
A lion or a bear,
He'd use his rod to strike the beast
And grab it by its hair.

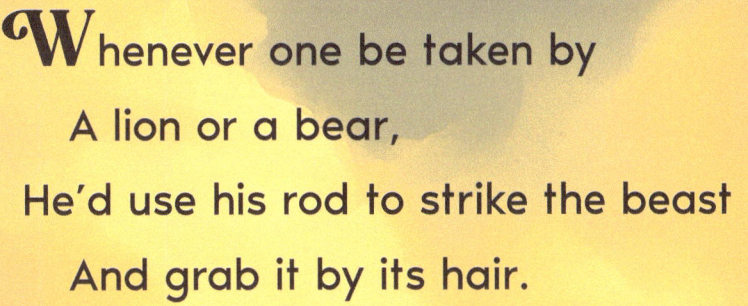

Read: 1 Sam 17:34-35

Then God one day to Jesse sent
His prophet Samuel
To find the one God chose to be
King over Israel.

First Jesse brought his oldest son,
"Not him," God's answer came.
And then he brought those next by age,
The answer, still the same.

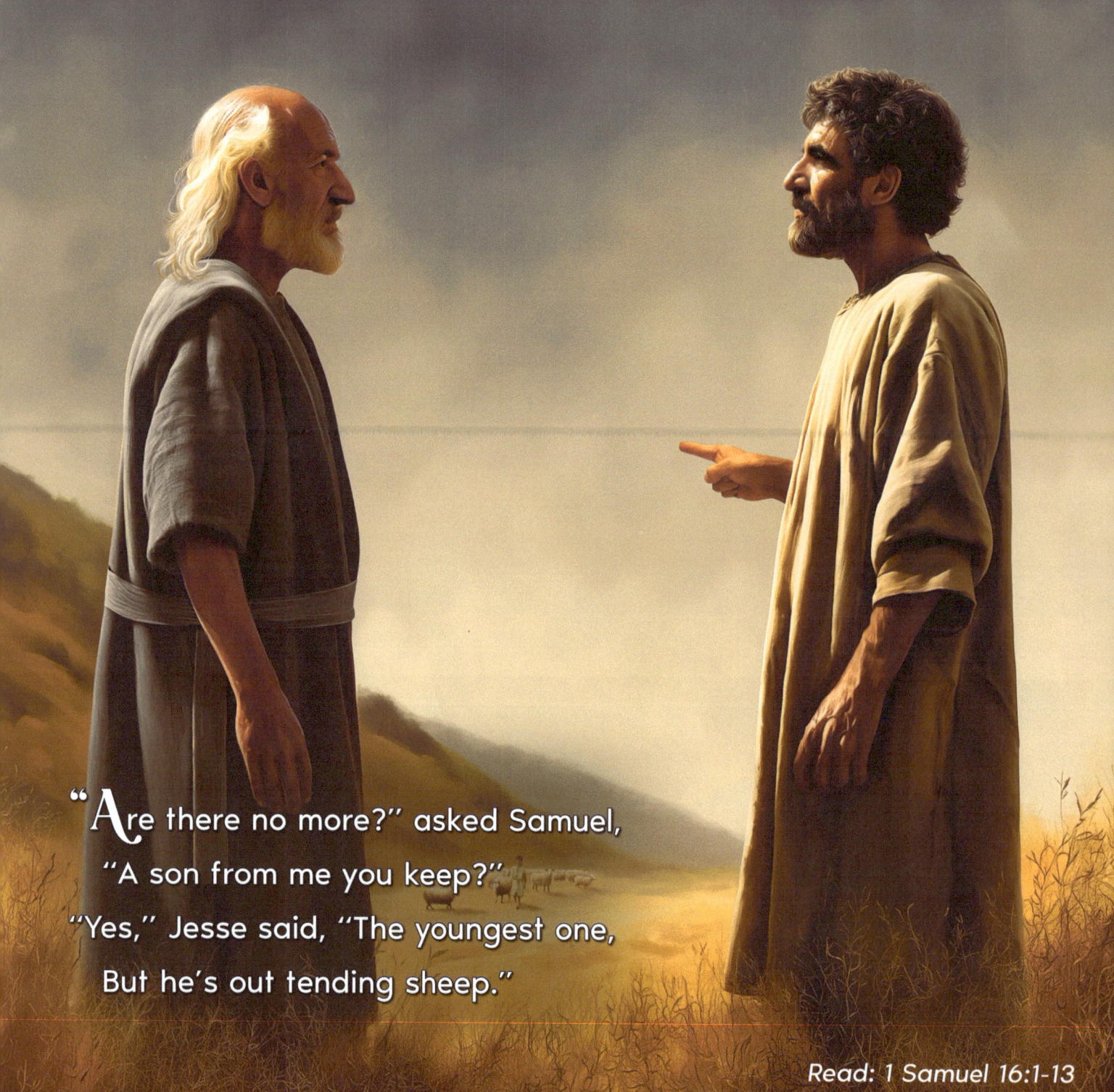

"Are there no more?" asked Samuel,
   "A son from me you keep?"
"Yes," Jesse said, "The youngest one,
   But he's out tending sheep."

Read: 1 Samuel 16:1-13

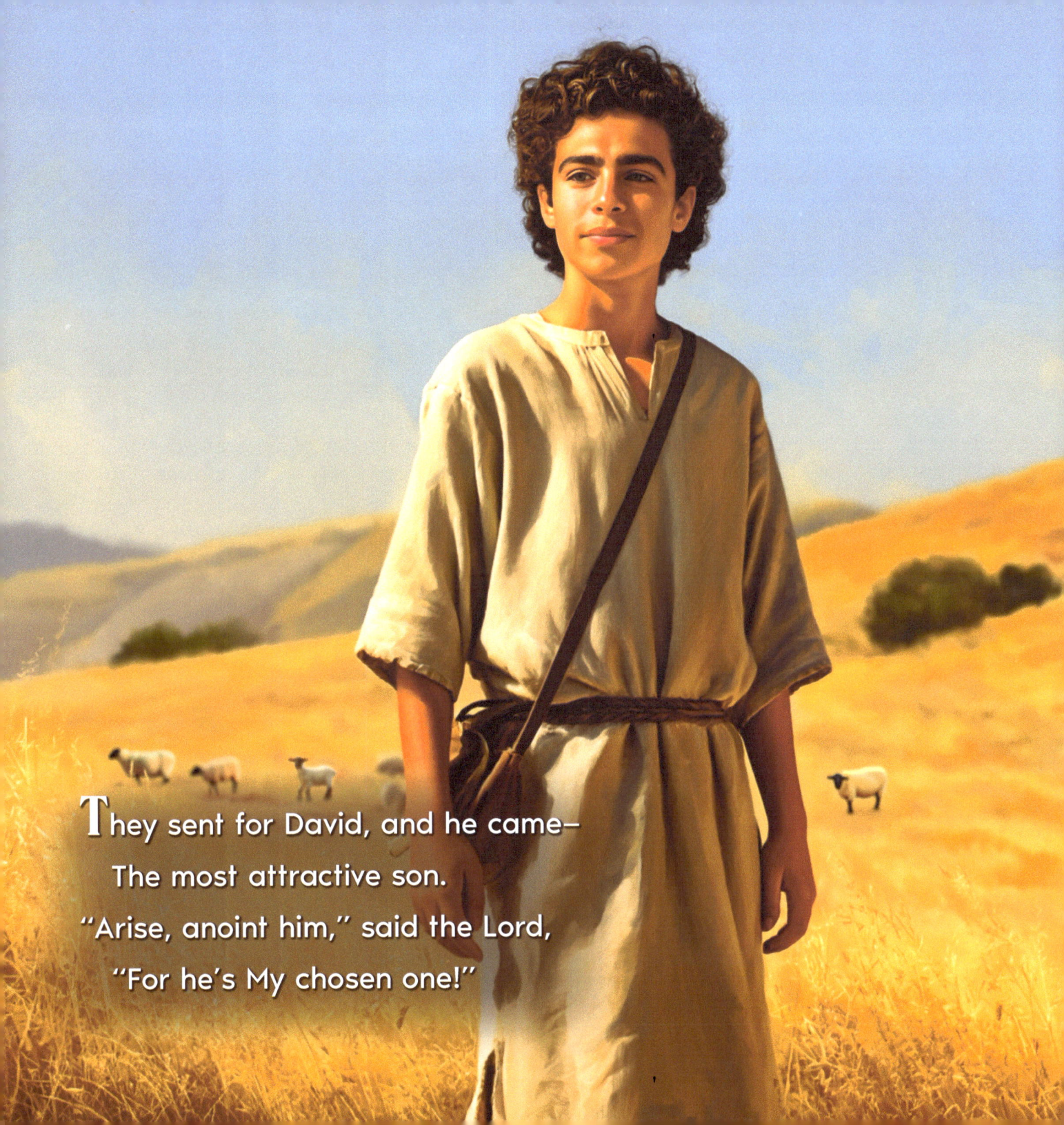

They sent for David, and he came—
The most attractive son.
"Arise, anoint him," said the Lord,
"For he's My chosen one!"

Read: 1 Samuel 16:13

So, over David, Samuel
   The holy oil outpoured.
And from that day, on David came
   The Spirit of the Lord.

Read: 1 Samuel 17:1-3

But soon God's people had to fight
　　Against the Philistines,
　Their armies gathered on two hills,
　　A valley in between.

The Israelites were terrorized
　　And filled with much despair,
　For there the huge Goliath stood
　　And mocked them with this dare:

"Come, send to me your strongest man,
Who's willing me to fight;
If he defeats me, then we'll all
Surrender here tonight!"

"But if I beat him, then you'll all
Submit to us today;
We will become your masters, and
Our orders you'll obey!"

When David heard Goliath's shout,
He said, "I now proclaim:
I've killed the lion and the bear,
To you I'll do the same!"

Read: 1 Sam. 17:4-11

Then, David put five rounded stones
  Into his shepherd's sack.
And forward with his sling he marched,
  Goliath to attack.

Read: 1 Samuel 17:40

Then David reaches in his sack,
One rounded stone takes now,
And from his sling he lets it fly,
Into Goliath's brow.

Goliath staggers and he falls
Right there at David's feet,
And David takes Goliath's sword
The vict'ry to complete.

Read: 1 Samuel 17:48-51

But David's strength was not within
His weapons nor his arm,
He trusted God to keep him safe
And never suffer harm.

God's blessing was on David, and
  The kingship he obtained.
He was a man of God's own heart;
  For forty years he reigned.

Read: 1 Samuel 13:14; 2 Samuel 5:4-5

Yet David was not perfect, he
Was just like us within.
For sometimes he would fall into
Unrighteousness and sin.

And when his conscience told him he'd
Done evil in God's sight,
He prayed that God forgive him, and
His sins as snow make white.

Read: Psalm 51

Through David's life, he always loved
To sing unto the Lord.
He wrote so many psalms and hymns,
His heart to God outpoured.

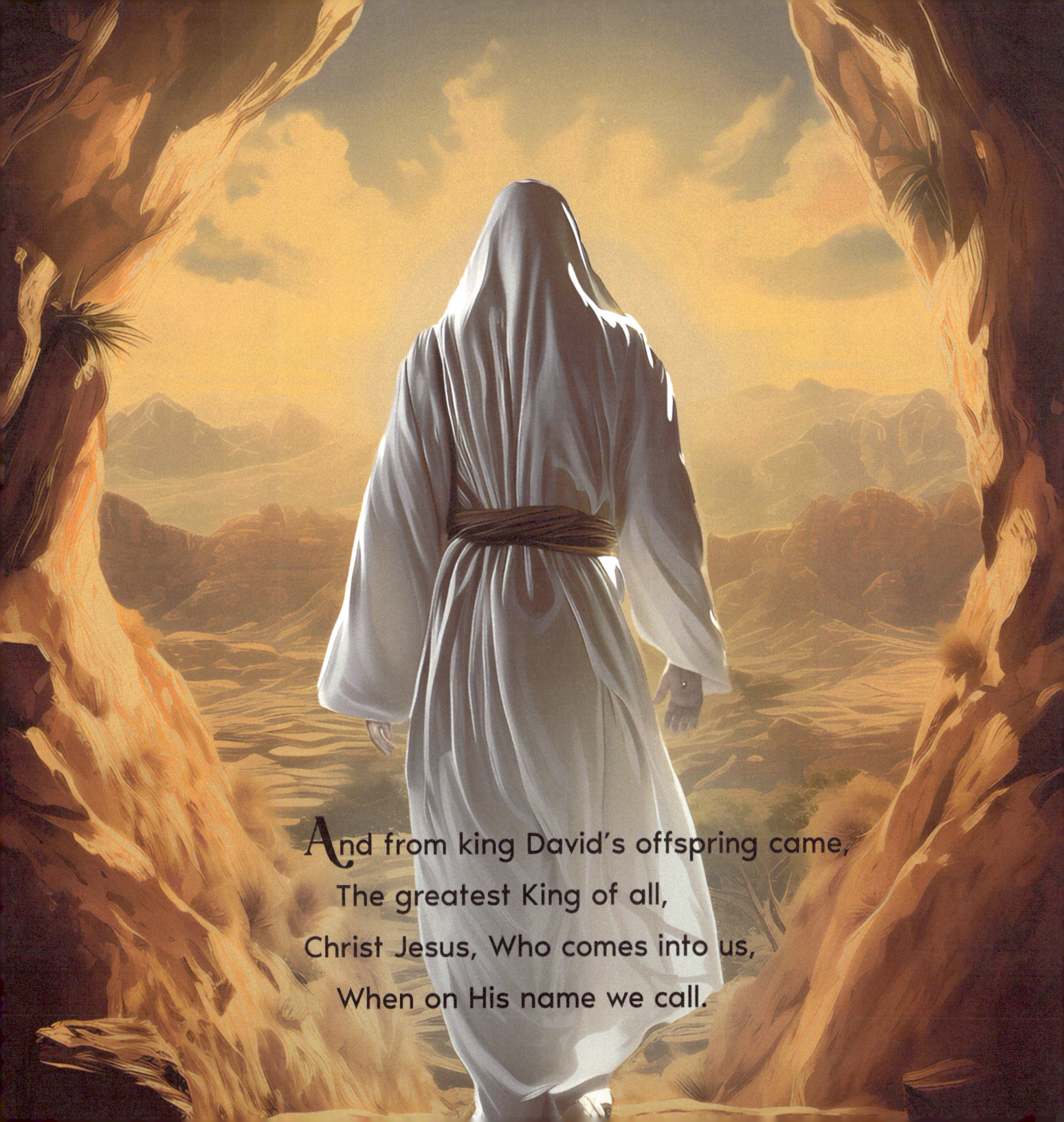

And from king David's offspring came,
The greatest King of all,
Christ Jesus, Who comes into us,
When on His name we call.

So, if like David, you desire
   For God to be your friend,
Just speak this prayer to Him out loud,
   Invite Him to come in.

Dear Jesus...
My Shepherd you are,
and I am your sheep,
Come into my heart,
my soul ever keep.
May Your Spirit now,
upon me be poured;
You are my best friend,
my Savior, my Lord.

Discussion Guide

WARRIOR HEART, SHEPHERD SPIRIT

Question: What made David someone who was both gentle toward others but also a fierce warrior?

Discuss: David had a soft heart for God and protected his father's little sheep. But he was also brave enough to fight dangerous animals and giants. True strength comes from loving God and protecting others. Ask your child if they can think of a time when they've had to be gentle with someone smaller and a time when they've had to be brave to protect or stand up for someone.

CHOSEN FOR CHARACTER, NOT SIZE

Question: Why did God pick the youngest brother?

Discuss: God saw David's loyal heart, not his youth. David's faithful work in small jobs showed his character. God looks for children faithful in everyday tasks. Ask your child how they can show God they're ready for bigger challenges. It's by being faithful in small things.

GOD AS OUR FRIEND

Question: How was God David's friend?

Discuss: Ask your child to name one of their friends. What is it like to have that person as a friend? For example, you talk a lot, share everything, and enjoy being together. This is how David was with God, sharing everything through songs and prayers. Ask your child if they can think of a time when they talked to God like a friend. What did they say?

STANDING WHEN OTHERS WON'T

Question: Why was David the only one willing to fight Goliath?

Discuss: All the grown-ups were scared, but David couldn't stand hearing God mocked. Sometimes we must stand for what's right when everyone else backs down. Discuss times your child might need to do what's right, even if others won't join them.

TRUSTING GOD'S STRENGTH

Question: How was David able to defeat such a giant?

Discuss: David didn't fight Goliath with his own strength: he trusted God to help. God's power won the battle. God helps us even if we're not the strongest or smartest. Ask your child about a time they needed God's help with something difficult.

ADMITTING WHEN YOU ARE WRONG

Question: What did David do when he made mistakes or did something wrong?

Discuss: Like all of us, David made some terrible choices, but he took responsibility and genuinely repented of his sin to God. Admitting mistakes shows strength. Discuss how admitting mistakes is a sign of maturity, and ask your child about a time they had to take responsibility and apologize.

A MAN AFTER GOD'S OWN HEART

Question: What does it mean that David was "a man after God's own heart"?

Discuss: This means David loved God and tried to honor and follow His ways, even when he did something wrong. God saw that David's deepest desire was to know and obey Him. It's about having a heart that genuinely seeks God and lives for Him. Ask your child: How can we show God that we want to have a heart that follows Him, just like David?

JESUS OUR GREATEST KING

Question: How does David's story point us to Jesus?

Discuss: David was a great king, but Jesus is the greatest King of all. Jesus is God's perfect chosen one, who can come into our hearts. We can invite Jesus to be our Shepherd and best friend. Ask your child if they would like Jesus to be their Shepherd and friend, and talk about what that means.

ROLE MODEL

Question: Which of David's qualities do you most want to develop?

Discuss: David showed courage, faithfulness, leadership, humility, and genuine friendship with God. These qualities made him a true hero. Encourage your child to pick one area to grow and discuss practical ways they can develop that in their daily life.

TO GET **FREE PRINTABLE DOWNLOADS** of the Discussion Guide and other free resources,
GO TO MY **WEBSITE:** WWW.ARABELLAPENROSE.COM

About the Series

At a time when boys often face confusion about what it means to be a man, the **Mighty Men of the Bible** series brings biblical role models to life for today's generation. Told in rhyming verse, each book shares the story of a different mighty man of the Bible, showcasing his unique character and strengths. The series features realistic illustrations that remind readers these are real men from real history—not fairy tales or made-up stories. By exploring the lives of men God intentionally chose to feature in His Word, young boys can discover godly examples of manhood and be encouraged to grow in courage, humility, leadership, and faith. Most importantly, they'll see that the very best role models for boys are found in the pages of the Bible. The faith-filled lives of these mighty men still speak powerfully to the hearts of boys today.

Looking for more Bible heroes?

Check out our companion series for girls:

REAL WOMEN HEROES OF THE BIBLE

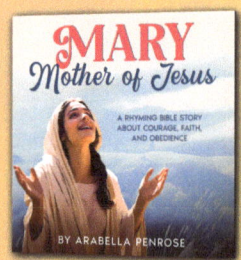 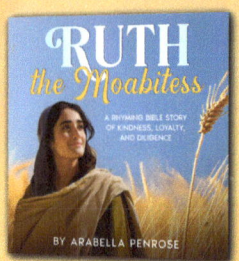 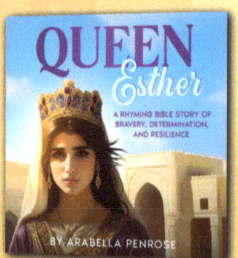 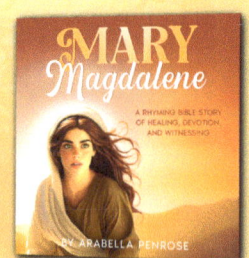 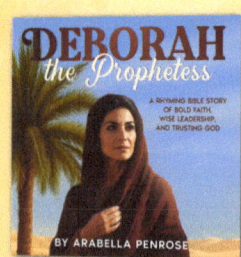

Two series. One mission.

Bringing biblical role models to life for today's generation.

TO GET UPDATES ON NEW RELEASES,

sign up for my newsletter at www.arabellapenrose.com

About the Author

Since childhood, Arabella has always loved poetry and dreamed of one day publishing her own poems. She splits her time between her native Southern California and Southern Spain. After earning her Bachelor of Arts from UC Santa Barbara, Arabella worked as a translator and a teacher. But her true passion is to nurture the hearts of children through stories. In her spare time, you can find Arabella hiking or walking the beach with her pup, Snoopy, and spending time with her son, Mateo. Arabella draws inspiration from her father, who instilled in her a love of poetry and scripture. She hopes to glorify God with her stories and inspire the next generation to discover the transformative power of God's Word.

Thank You!

Dear reader,

I hope reading this rhyming bible story inspired you and your child as much as it did me in writing it.

If you found value in this book, please consider leaving an honest review on Amazon or Goodreads. Your feedback helps other families discover meaningful books. And, by sharing your thoughts, you encourage me to continue writing stories that nurture little hearts.

Thank you for reading this timeless tale of David with your child. I'm grateful for readers like you.

Blessings,

Arabella Penrose

HAVE A PRAYER REQUEST
or want to reach out? Email me at
arabella@arabellapenrose.com

www.ingramcontent.com/pod-product-compliance
Lightning Source LLC
Chambersburg PA
CBHW041405010526
44107CB00015B/1082